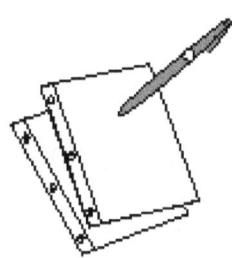

Power Hitter® Classroom Language Arts

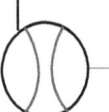

POWER HITTER® LANGUAGE ARTS BOOK 1
Veltri, Barbara Torre
ISBN 978-0-9794020-2-8

All rights reserved.
Reproduction in whole or in part, electronically or in digital files is prohibited.
Baseball and Softball characters are registered trademarks with USPTO.

© 2001-2024 Barbara Torre Veltri, Ed. D All rights reserved

Power Hitter® Language Arts Book 1
Table of Contents

The Tale of the Home Room Ball!..pg. 1

Nouns: Common and Proper... pg. 2

Minor and Major League Nouns... pg. 3

Plural Nouns.. pg. 4

Noun Wave.. pg. 5

Verbs: Baseball's Action Words...pg. 6

Verb Tenses...pg. 7

Verbs: Recap...pg. 8

Adverbs...pg. 9

Adjectives..pg. 10

Prepositions.. pg. 11

Punctuation Marks. . ?... pg. 12

Punctuation Marks: !, ( )... pg. 13

Comma.. pg. 14

Apostrophe.. pg. 15

Quotation Marks... pg. 16

Fix the Sports Quotes... pg. 17

Proofreading... pg. 18

You Make the Call (Usage).. pg. 19

Metaphors... pg. 20

Similes... pg. 21

Alliteration... pg. 22

Personification... pg. 23

You Make the Call! (Recap)... pg. 24

© 2001-2024 Barbara Torre Veltri, Ed. D. All rights reserved. www.powerhitter.com

Power Hitter® Language Arts
The Tale of the Home Run Ball!

Name   Game Day

Pre-Game Info:
Pretend that you are the home run ball hit out of the park. What does it feel like when a hitter's bat sends you flying into the air? Where do you land? Who finds you? Tell about your adventures...

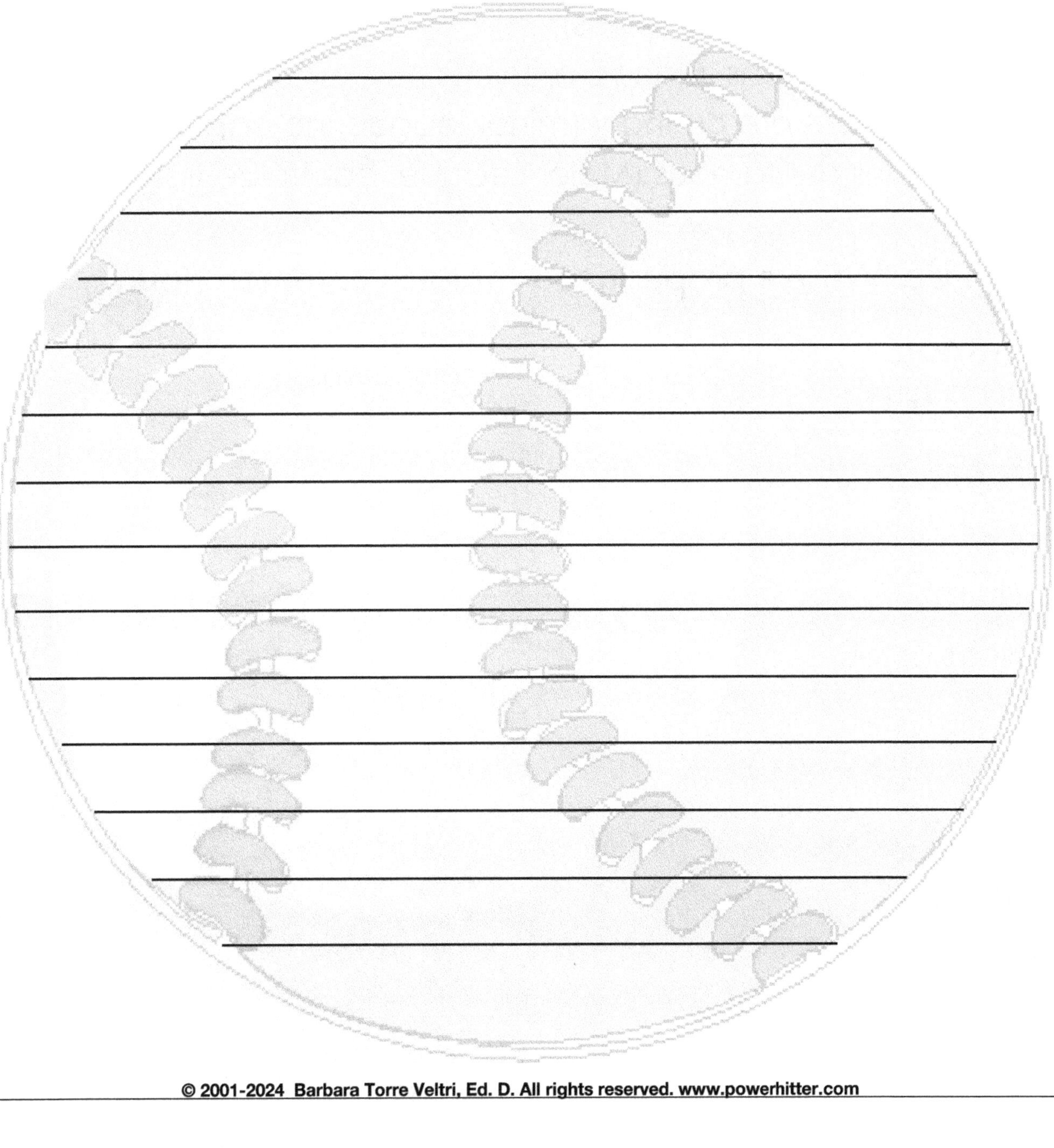

_____

_____

_____

_____

_____

_____

_____

_____

_____

_____

_____

_____

Power Hitter® Language Arts
Nouns: Common/Proper

Name _____ Game Day

Pre-Game Info: We use parts of speech in reading and writing. They are like position players in a game!
Nouns (player and team members)
Verbs (action words)
Adjectives/Adverbs (describing words)
Prepositions (directional words)
Nouns name persons, places, or things.
Common Nouns are ordinary (minor league, no capitalization).
Proper Nouns are famous (Major League, capitalize first letter).

You're Up: Write a proper noun for each common noun.

Common (minor league)	**Proper** (Major League)
baseball	1. _____
player	2. _____
stadium	3. _____
mascot	4. _____
city	5. _____
state	6. _____
song	7. _____
manager	8. _____
owner	9. _____
team	

© 2001-2004 Barbara Torre Veltri, Ed. D. All rights reserved. Powerhitter LLC

Power Hitter® Language Arts
Nouns

Name _____   Game Day _____

You're Up! Create your own list that moves from the minors to the majors. Remember, Major League nouns (proper) lead off with a capital letter!

Minor League (common nouns)	**Major League** (proper nouns)
1.	
2.	
3.	
4.	
5.	
6.	
7.	
8.	
9.	
10.	

Power Hitter® Language Arts
Plural Nouns

Name _____ Game Day

Pre-Game Info: Nouns name a person, place or thing. Nouns can be a player (singular), or an entire team (plural). When you talk about more than one, or **plural**, you need to add endings such as **s, es, or ies.**
Remember: Don't use an apostrophe ' with plural nouns.

For most nouns you can just **add (s)**   example: bat + s = bats

But, when a word ends in **ch, sh,** or **x,** you need to **add (es)**

example: catch + **es** = catches

When a word ends in **y**, following a consonant, drop the y, and **add (ies)** example: party - y + **ies** = parties

You're Up! Write the plural of each noun below.

Singular   **Plural**

player   = _____
bench   = _____
miss   = _____
pitch   = _____
righty   = _____

Sometimes a pitcher throws a few curves at you. Can you still connect, and think of the plural form of nouns that don't follow the game plan above?

Singular   Plural

man   _____
person   _____
child   _____
house   _____
lady   _____

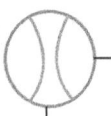
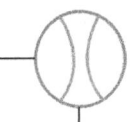

Power Hitter® Language Arts
Noun Wave

Name   Game Day

Pre-Game Info: Create a Noun Wave! It's simple!
Look at the noun listed in each row next to the number 1. Circle the last letter of each noun and use it to make a new noun.

Example: 1. Glov(e)
            2. Erro(r)
            3. Rightfielder

1. Ba<u>t</u>	1. Hotdo<u>g</u>	1. Moun<u>d</u>
2. T	2. G	2. D
3. _____	3. _____	3. _____
4. _____	4. _____	4. _____
5. _____	5. _____	5. _____
6. _____	6. _____	6. _____
7. _____	7. _____	7. _____
8. _____	8. _____	8. _____
9. _____	9. _____	9. _____
10. _____	10. _____	10. _____

© 2001--2024 Barbara Torre Veltri, Ed. D. All rights reserved. www.powerhitter.com

Power Hitter® Language Arts
Verbs - Baseball's Action Words

Name _____ Game Day _____

Pre-Game Info: Verbs are action, "What's happening?" words! Verbs are always doing something! Nouns and verbs work like a pitcher and a catcher!

Here's an example:

Shoehai Ohtani **hit** over 55 home runs

and **stole** over 55 bases this year!

You're Up! Write a sentence using:

Verbs in the Bullpen

pitch	catch	collide
slide	leap	yell

1. _____

2. _____

3. _____

4. _____

5. _____

6. _____

© 2001-2024 Barbara Torre Veltri, Ed. D. All rights reserved. Powerhitter LLC

Power Hitter® Language Arts
Verb Tenses

Name   Game Day

Pre-Game Info: We already know that verbs are action words. **Jump, leap, fly, yell, slide** are examples of verbs. Verbs tell us when the action takes place.

Is it happening now?..present
Did it happen already?..past
Will it happen later?...future

Verbs change form, similar to the way athletes change uniforms for home and away games. We call these verb changes, **tenses: present, past, and future.**

If action happens now, it's **present tense**:

Alex **plays** shortstop.

If the action happened, it's **past tense**:

Alex **played** shortstop yesterday.

If the action will happen, it's **future tense**:

Alex **will play** shortstop tomorrow.

You're up! Locate an article in the sports section (newspaper or internet) and find 10 verbs that are past tense, present tense, and future tense. Write them on the lines below.

1._____   6._____
2._____   7._____
3._____   8._____
4._____   9._____
5._____   10._____

© 2001-2024 Barbara Torre Veltri, Ed. D. All rights reserved. www.Powerhitter.com

Power Hitter® Language Arts
Verb Recap

Name _____ Game Day _____

Underline the verbs in the sentences below.

1. The ball flew out of the ball park.
2. The umpire yelled, "Play ball!"
3. Fans screamed and jumped for joy.
4. The team ran from the dugout.
5. The cameraman recorded the scene.
6. Sportswriters were writing furiously.

YOU'RE UP!

Write 5 sentences using verb tenses.

1. _____
2. _____
3. _____
4. _____
5. _____

Power Hitter® Language Arts
Adverbs

Name _____   Game Day _____

Adverbs are like the reporters at the game. They tell how, when, and where. They team up with verbs. Most adverbs end with the suffix, ly or ness.

HOW DID THE ALL-STAR RUN AFTER HE BLASTED THE BALL?
confidently   slowly   intently   proudly   jubilantly

YOU'RE UP!
Write 5 sentences that include adverbs. Underline them.

1. _____
2. _____
3. _____
4. _____
5. _____

Power Hitter® Language Arts
Adjectives

_____   _____
Name   Game Day

Pre-Game Info: Adjectives are describing words that are teammates of nouns.

<u>Here's an example</u>: That was an **exciting** play.

You're Up! Use adjectives to describe:

    A DAY AT THE BALL PARK

Divide your ideas into categories or topics!

Weather	Scenery
1. _____	_____
2. _____	_____
3. _____	_____
4. _____	_____
5. _____	_____

Power Hitter® Language Arts
Prepositions

Name _____ Game Day _____

Pre-Game Info: Prepositions are little words that hold the team or sentence together! They are like catchers who set up the pitch, by connecting nouns, verbs, adjectives, adverbs -- the entire parts of speech team!

YOU'RE UP! Can you identify the preposition in these phrases at the Ball Park?

THE PITCH... THE HIT... WHERE DID THE BALL GO?

over the base _____

under his foot _____

across the diamond _____

near the bullpen _____

into right field _____

above the bleachers _____

underneath the stands _____

by the photographer _____

next to the dugout _____

Power Hitter® Language Arts
Punctuation Marks can be : . ? ! ' , " " (?)

Name _____ Game Day

Pre-Game Info: Punctuation marks are really signs. They tell you to pause, stop, question, or show emotion when you are reading and writing. Can you imagine if there were no signs on a page of writing? The words would go on and on. It would be like a ball game that never ends!!! Signs in baseball tell the players what to do. Signs in written language, are called punctuation marks and can look like this:

. ? ! ' , " " ( ) :

A period sentence tells something (.)
Example: Kenny plays centerfield.

You're up: Write a sentence that tells something.

_____

_____

A period sentence can be a command (.)
Example: Stretch first, and then run two laps.

You're up: Write a sentence that gives a command.

_____

_____

A question mark (?) is used as a closer when asking a question.
Example: Can your team win it all this year?

You're up: Can you write a sentence that asks a question?.

_____

_____

© 2001-2024 Barbara Torre Veltri, Ed. D All rights reserved.

Power Hitter® Language Arts
Punctuation marks can be : . ? ! ' , " " ( )

Name _____ Game Day _____

Pre-Game Info: An **exclamation ! point** is used as a closer when a strong feeling or emotion is expressed.

    Example: It's going, going, -- it's out of here!

You're Up! Write a sentence that shows emotion.

_____

_____

Parentheses ( ) are a **pair** of curved lines used to set apart words, phrases, or numbers within a sentence (not necessary but helpful).

Example: Jones (15-7) will oppose Ohtani (12-4) in tonight's game.

    You're Up! Write a sentence with parenthesis .

_____

_____

A **Colon :** is used before a long series of words, a quotation hour/minute or ratio.
Example: The game begins at 7: 05 p.m.

    You're Up! Write a sentence with a colon.

_____

_____

© 2001-2024 Barbara Torre Veltri, Ed. D. All rights reserved.

Power Hitter® Language Arts
Punctuation Marks can be : . ? ! ' , " " ( ) ;

Name _____ Game Day _____

Pre-Game Info: A Comma is a mark that separates words in a sentence. Commas give you a break between words so that the sentence makes sense. They're like breaks in-between innings. Commas are used to separate a series of words, or a city and a state.

Example: Keisha ate cracker jacks, a hot dog, and a pretzel.

You're Up! Write a sentence that uses a comma to separate words in a series.

_____

_____

Example: Is Baseball's Hall of Fame in Cooperstown, NY?

You're Up! Write a sentence that uses a comma to separate city and state.

_____

_____

Commas are also used in direct address, which is a way to identify the person you are speaking about, and add a bit of extra information.

Example: Lou, our manager, played for the Yankees.

You're Up! Write a sentence that uses a comma in direct address.

_____

_____

Power Hitter® Language Arts
Punctuation Marks can be : . ? ! ' , " " ( ) ;

_____   _____
Name   Game Day

Pre-Game Info: An Apostrophe (a-pos-tro-phe) is a comma in the sky! (') It takes the place of a missing letter. We use an apostrophe with contractions, when we omit (take out) letters, like the way a ball player is taken out of a line-up.

Here's what we mean.

Contractions are short cuts. Here, the apostrophe (') is used in place of a letter.

You're Up! Look at the examples below. Which letter does the apostrophe replace?

He didn't (did not) see the sign.   _____
                                                              missing letter

Joey's (Joey is) the lead off hitter.   _____
                                                              missing letter

He couldn't (could not) see the ball.   _____
                                                              missing letter

The umpire said, "You're (you are) out!" _____
                                                              missing letter

You're up! Write a sentence with a contraction and apostrophe.

_____

_____

_____

_____

Power Hitter® Language Arts
Punctuation Marks can be: . ? ! ' , " " ( ) ;

Pre-Game Info: Quotation Marks (" ") surround the exact words of a speaker. Remember to capitalize the first letter of the word that begins the quote.

Here's an example:
"Can I have your autograph?" asked the fan.

Insert quotation marks for the sentences below.

    I'm just trying to help the team, stated the player.
    You're out! shouted the umpire.

You're Up! Write a sentence that uses quotation marks to identify a speaker's words.

_____

_____

We also use quotation marks to identify titles of published work, like songs, articles, and sayings.

The fans sang, "Take Me Out to the Ball Game" during the 7th inning stretch.

You're up! Write a sentence that uses quotation marks for a song title.

_____

_____

Power Hitter® Language Arts
Fix the Sports' Quotes

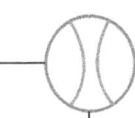

Name _____   Game Day _____

Pre-Game Info: Sportswriters interview players, coaches, and fans to include quotes in their stories! Their deadline is one hour after the game's conclusion. The story must be written and error free before it's printed. Quotation marks (" ") enclose the exact words of each speaker.

You're Up! There are several errors in the quotes below. Put an X on the mistake and rewrite the corrected version on the lines.

Hint: Look for misspelled words, and errors in punctuation, and capitalization.

1. we one because this teem came to play today

   _____

2. it ain't over 'til its over stated ny yankee yogi berra

   _____

3. we'll get them tomorrow team said the coach

   _____

4. we will we will rock you sang the fans

   _____

5. i through him a ball low and inside i guess he just got a peace of it

   _____

6. alana was incredible! she scored ate runs and had to assists.

   _____

© 2001-2024 Barbara Torre Veltri, Ed. D All rights reserved.

Power Hitter® Language Arts Proofreading

Name   Game Day

Pre-Game Info: Sportswriters describe events on the field. Proofreading is part of their game plan! Look for punctuation, capitalization and spelling errors.

You're Up! Can you help the Sportswriter Fix the Sentence below?

the philadelphia phillies the new york mets the atlanta braves the miami marlins and the washington nationals play in the eastern division of the national league

_____

_____

_____

_____

Write your own error sentence. Have a teammate edit it for you.

_____

_____

_____

_____

Power Hitter® Language Arts
Correct Usage

Name _____ Game Day _____

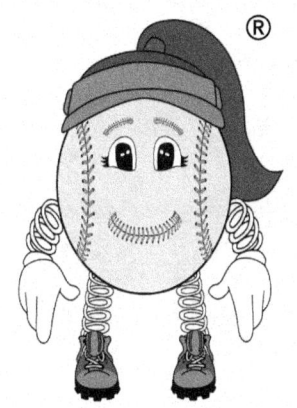

You Make the Call!

You're Up! Help the umpire make the call. Circle the correct choice in each sentence.

1. He (been hitting, has been hitting, be hitting) in the leadoff position.

2. The manager (had played, played, plays) for the Yankees.

3. Alec is (are, our) shortstop.

4. He was (born, borned) in New York City.

5. The mascot is over (their, there, they're.)

6. The team (won, one) today.

7. Liv (seen, saw, see) me play.

8. She (went, gone, go) to the souvenir stand.

9. The telephone in the bullpen (rang, rung, ring.)

19

© 2001-2024 Barbara Torre Veltri, Ed. D. All rights reserved.

Power Hitter® Language Arts
Metaphors

Name _____ Game Day

Pre-Game Info: Metaphors describe an object through comparison.

Here's an example: Wow! Luis caught a rocket!

Hint: The sharpness of the hit caused the ball to be described as a rocket. It's still a ball!

You're Up!
Can you write 4 metaphors?

1. _____

2. _____

3. _____

4. _____

© 2001-2024 Barbara Torre Veltri, Ed. D. All rights reserved.

Power Hitter® Language Arts
Similies

Name _____ Game Day

Pre-Game Info: A Simile (ˈsɪm əl i) compares dissimilar things/people using "like" or "as."

Here's an example:
"Aaron doesn't feel pressure. He's <u>as</u> cool <u>as</u> a cucumber."

You're Up!
Write 4 phrases that use a SIMILE and raise your batting average!

1.

2. _____

3. _____

4. _____

Power Hitter® Language Arts
Alliteration

Name Game Day

Pre-Game Info: Alliteration is the repetition of beginning consonants.

Here's an example: Harper hits homers.

The consonant **H** is repeated.

You're Up!

Use alliteration in your 4 trips to the plate!

1. _____

2. _____

3. _____

4. _____

Power Hitter® Language Arts
Personification

Name _____ Game Day

Pre-Game Info: Personification gives lifeless objects human qualities or form.

Here's an example: That ball **flew** out of here!

Hint: Balls don't fly. In real life, does the ball have wings?

You're Up!
Write 4 phrases that use personification.

1. _____

2. _____

3. _____

4. _____

© 2001-2024 Barbara Torre Veltri, Ed. D. All rights reserved.

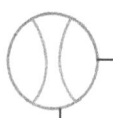 

Power Hitter® Language Arts
You Make The Call...

Name _____   Game Day _____

Pre-Game Warm-Up: Sportswriters use figurative language, to provide a picture of what's happening on and off the field.

You're Up! Read each sentence below. If the writer uses:

Alliteration, repeating consonants for effect,   **write A**

Metaphor, describing an object by comparison or analogy.   **write M**

Personification, giving human qualities to objects or non-human form.   **write P**

Similes, comparing dissimilar things using "like" or "as,"   **write S**

1. Randy fires the ball at 100 m.p.h   _____

2. Alex is as slick as a lollipop.   _____

3. Brett's bat blasts balls beyond bleachers.   _____

4. Lizzie's ball slices towards the left field line.   _____

5. Sally flew to first base.   _____

6. Janie throws heat!   _____

7. Edgar connects like puzzle pieces.   _____

8. Pop pleads, "Pitch perfectly, please!"   _____

9. J.T.s throw is on the money.   _____

© 2001-2024 Barbara Torre Veltri, Ed. D. All rights reserved.

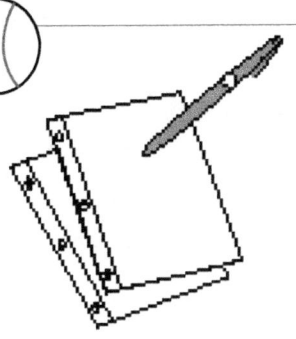

Power Hitter®Classroom
Language Arts
Notes

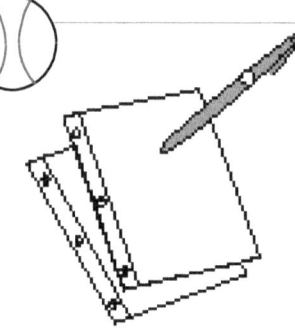

Power Hitter® Classroom
Language Arts

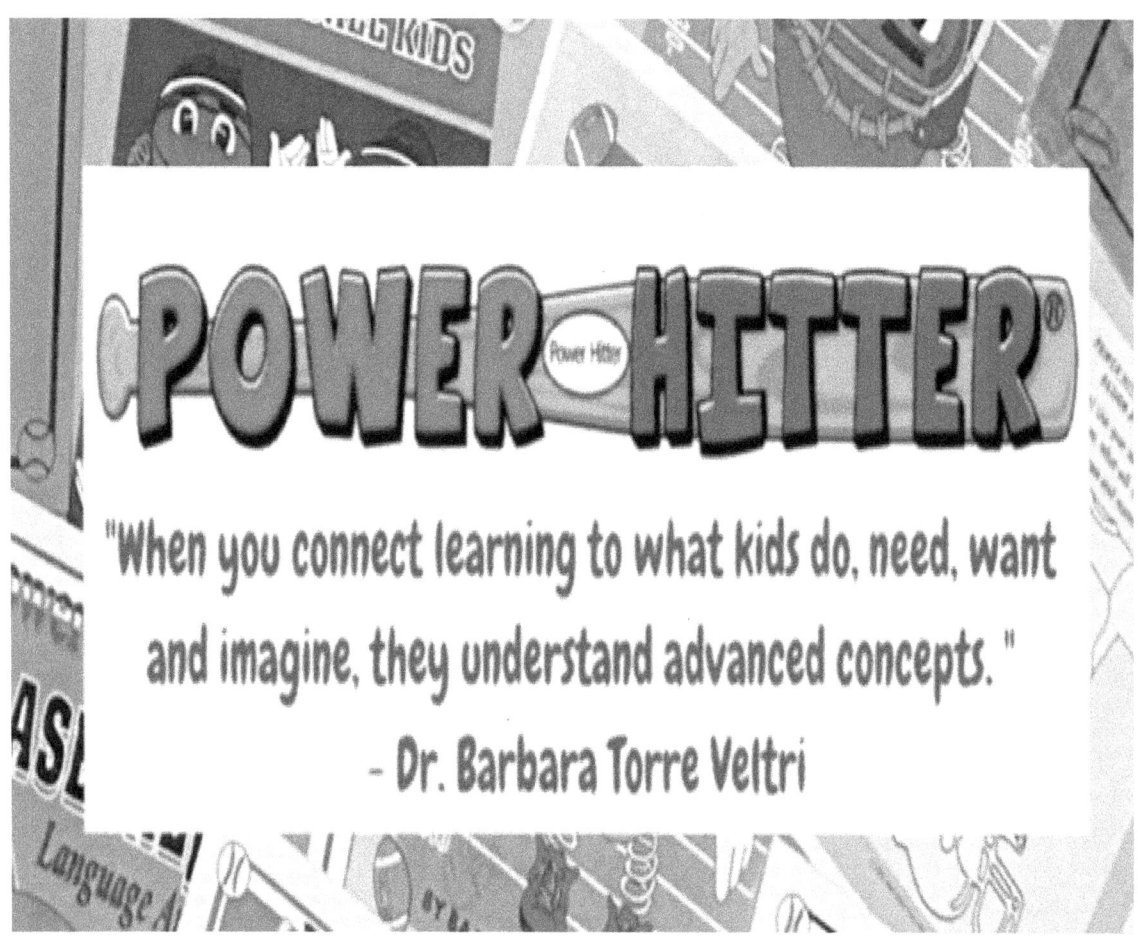

"When you connect learning to what kids do, need, want and imagine, they understand advanced concepts."
— Dr. Barbara Torre Veltri

Hope your day's a Winner!

Sincerely,

Barbara Torre Veltri

Dr. Barbara Torre Veltri, Creator/CEO
Powerhitter LLC
www.powerhitter.com

© 2021-2024 Barbara Torre Veltri, Ed. D All rights reserved

www.ingramcontent.com/pod-product-compliance
Lightning Source LLC
LaVergne TN
LVHW061326060426
835510LV00017B/1945